For all the little
stargazers around the
world, looking up at the
sky we share. – *Rola Shaw*

For Hattie. – *Lara Hawthorne*

First published in Great Britain 2021 by Red Shed,
part of Farshore

An imprint of HarperCollins*Publishers*
1 London Bridge Street,
London SE1 9GF

www.farshore.co.uk

HarperCollins*Publishers*
1st Floor, Watermarque Building, Ringsend Road
Dublin 4, Ireland

Text copyright © HarperCollins*Publishers* Limited 2021
Written by Rola Shaw, pen name for AHA Creates

Illustrations copyright © Lara Hawthorne 2021
Lara Hawthorne has asserted her moral rights.

ISBN 978 1 4052 9778 3
Printed in China.
001

Consultancy by Carole Stott

Night Sky

Written by Rola Shaw

Illustrated by Lara Hawthorne

RED SHED

The Night Sky

Long, long ago the stars shone brightly in the night sky. They glimmered over the dinosaurs, just as they shine over us today. These glowing specks of light are great, blazing balls of gas, trillions of kilometres away in space. Some stars seem brighter than others because they are closer to Earth. Other stars beam brightly because they are hotter and give off more light.

Constellations

The night sky shimmers with stars that seem to move in fixed patterns, which we call constellations. There are 88 constellations in the sky surrounding Earth. In Europe and other places north of the Equator, we see the stars and constellations of the Northern Hemisphere. South of the Equator, in places like Australia, the constellations of the Southern Hemisphere shine.

The Moon is the brightest object in the night sky.

For thousands of years, we have used the stars to predict the seasons, to understand how time works, and to guide us on long journeys over land and sea. The stars have given storytellers a canvas for our myths and legends too.

The Milky Way

Huge fields of spinning stars and planets exist together in our galaxy, which is called the Milky Way. On a clear, dark night, you can see the Milky Way. It looks like a gigantic, pale smudge, streaked across the dark sky. The Milky Way is just one of billions of galaxies in the Universe!

The Southern Cross

The Southern Cross

South of the Equator, you can see Crux, or the Southern Cross, which is the smallest of all the constellations. The Venda and Sotho peoples of southern Africa imagine its bright stars to be two giraffes crossing in the sky.

Some African dung beetles roll balls of elephant poo in a straight line. They use patterns of light from the Milky Way to guide them. The scurrying beetles eat the dung, or bury it along with their eggs. When the eggs hatch the baby beetles eat the dung.

Kalahari Tale

There are many tales told across the world of how the Milky Way came to be. In the Kalahari desert of southern Africa, the Khoisan people say a young girl made a path of stars in the darkness by flinging glowing embers and fire ash into the sky.

Early Farmers

Thousands of years ago, there was no such thing as a clock or a calendar. How was anyone to know if it was spring, summer, autumn or winter? The weather can be full of tricks! A warm spell in winter is not a good time to plant seeds. People learned to watch the changing star patterns, so they could predict the seasons, and plant at the right time.

On a spring night, the Plough appears upside down, high in the northern sky.

On a winter night, the handle of the Plough tilts towards the ground.

The Plough

In the Northern Hemisphere, a pattern of seven stars forms the Plough. Its position changes with the seasons but it is easy to find thanks to its long 'handle' and large 'bowl'. The Plough is an asterism, which means it is part of a larger constellation.

The Teapot

In the Southern Hemisphere, in the constellation of Sagittarius, you can see a pattern of eight stars called the Teapot. In winter, it is high in the sky all night long. When you see the Teapot, you are looking directly towards the centre of the Milky Way.

On a summer night, the Plough's handle points away from the ground.

On an autumn night, the Plough appears the right way up, low in the northern sky.

Ancient Egyptians

The ancient Egyptians loved to gaze at the stars. Every year they watched for Sirius (the brightest star in the night sky), waiting for it to rise just before daybreak. When it did, they knew the River Nile would soon flood and crops would grow. The flooding of the Nile marked the beginning of the ancient Egyptian year and was a time of celebration.

Canis Major and Orion

Sirius is part of the constellation Canis Major, which means 'big dog' in Latin.

Orion

Canis Major

Sirius

Canis Major follows Orion the Hunter across the sky.

The Book of Nut

The ancient Egyptians worshipped Nut – the goddess of the sky, the Universe and of mothers. The Egyptians believed that Nut's body stretched over the whole Earth, creating the sky. They said that every night, Nut swallowed the Sun and gave birth to it again the following morning. The *Book of Nut* is full of stories about the night sky and the movement of the Sun, Moon and the planets.

The Pyramids of Giza

These ancient burial tombs were built for Egyptian kings, called pharaohs. Architects and astronomers used the position of the Sun and stars to plan their location precisely, so that the sides of the pyramids lined up perfectly with the points of the compass: north, south, east and west.

The pyramids of Giza are roughly 4,500 years old.

Ancient Greeks

There were a great many storytellers and scientists in ancient Greece. In the second century, a brilliant astronomer and mathematician called Ptolemy studied the night sky. He recorded 48 of the 88 constellations we have today, naming them after stories and characters from Greek myths and legends.

North Star

Ursa Major

In the Latin language, Ursa Major means 'great bear'. This is the largest constellation in the Northern Hemisphere and it includes the Plough. Look carefully and you will see two stars from the bowl of the Plough, pointing to Polaris, the North Star.

Hypatia of Alexandria, one of the first female scientists, was a gifted astronomer and mathematician.

Draco and Hercules

These constellations show the Greek hero Hercules with his foot on the head of Draco, which means 'dragon' in Latin. In this myth, Hercules defeats the dragon that guards the golden apples in the Garden of the Hesperides. It is one of many Greek stories that can be seen in the stars.

The ancient Greeks invented instruments such as the armillary sphere to help them track the positions of the stars and planets.

Ancient China

The Chinese believed that events in the night sky mirrored life on Earth. A comet or an eclipse could be a sign of war or famine to come! It was the responsibility of astronomers working at the imperial court to record the movements of the Sun, Moon and stars, and advise the emperor what might happen.

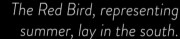

The emperor was believed to be the son of heaven.

The Blue Dragon, representing spring, lay in the east, which was shown on the left on early Chinese maps.

The Red Bird, representing summer, lay in the south.

Palaces in the Sky

Astronomers split the sky into five regions, called 'palaces', or 'gong' in Chinese. The most important gong represented the Emperor and his household. The rest of the sky was divided into the points of the compass: north, south, east and west.

The Black Tortoise, representing winter, lay in the north.

The White Tiger, representing autumn, lay in the west.

Chinese Astronomers

During the Song Dynasty (960–1279) many observatories were built so that the emperor's astronomers could watch the stars, planets and constellations, and advise him. Chinese astronomers invented incredibly accurate tools to measure time and even learned to predict unusual events such as comets and meteor showers.

The Gaocheng Astronomical Observatory was built in 1276.

Guo Shoujing

An important Chinese astronomer was Guo Shoujing. He built a large stone observatory at Gaocheng where he measured the angle of the Sun's shadow to determine the seasons. In 1280, he calculated the length of a year to within 26 seconds of the actual length, and so created an accurate calendar.

A Scientific Explosion

In 1609, an Italian astronomer named Galileo Galilei turned his telescope up towards the skies above Padua. He was amazed to see the craters that prick the Moon, and the mountains that rise above its rocky surface. Before long, other astronomers were exploring the night sky – a scientific revolution had begun!

Galileo's Telescope

Galileo was the first person to use a telescope to study the night sky and record what he saw. He realised that the path of light in the sky, which we call the Milky Way, is made up of a vast number of individual stars.

Copernicus

Around 70 years before Galileo, a Polish astronomer named Copernicus claimed that the Sun lies at the centre of our Solar System, and that Earth and all the planets travel around it. Most people didn't believe Copernicus, but Galileo proved he was right.

Isaac Newton

Thanks to Galileo's discoveries, astronomers worked out the size of the planets and the speed at which they move around the Sun. In 1687, English astronomer Isaac Newton discovered the amazing force that keeps the planets moving around the Sun, and which holds everything in the Solar System together – gravity!

Saturn

Venus

Sun

Mercury

Jupiter

Mars

Earth

These are the planets and the Sun, almost as Galileo observed them with his telescope.

Navigation

Far out to sea, where waves rise and fall, a journey can be long and perilous and the waters unknown. Sailors need to know exactly where they are, and for thousands of years they plotted their course and discovered new lands following the positions and movements of the stars.

Ancient Star Maps

Early Polynesian sailors were incredible navigators, criss-crossing the Pacific Ocean using the stars. First they pinpointed a star lying close to the horizon, and sailed towards it. They switched to a second star when the first had risen higher in the sky. Sailors memorised sequences of stars for each route, creating a star map. Many sailors still use these traditional Polynesian methods today.

Polynesian boat

The Compass

By 1100, the Chinese had invented one of the most important navigation tools – the magnetic compass. The magnetised needle of the compass lines up with Earth's poles, telling a sailor which way is north.

Finding Latitude

Sailors continued to use the stars and the compass to navigate and explore, but the invention of the sextant in the 18th century opened up new possibilites. A sextant tells a sailor how far north or south they have travelled. This is called latitude. In 1768, Captain Cook sailed from England to Tahiti using this new invention.

A sextant measures the angle between the horizon and the Moon, or a star or planet.

Captain Cook's ship, HMS *Endeavour*.

The Global Positioning System

Today, sailors use GPS to navigate, instead of stars. GPS bounces radio waves off satellites that orbit Earth. In 2011, Laura Dekker set off to become the youngest person to sail around the world single-handed. Laura used GPS but she carried a sextant and ocean charts, in case the technology failed.

Satellites orbiting Earth are part of the GPS.

Laura Dekker's boat, Guppy.

Modern Astronomy

Antarctica is a vast, cold and icy place, but the night sky is perhaps clearer than anywhere else on Earth. Here you'll find the South Pole Telescope – a super powerful telescope that can see incredible distances into our galaxy, the Milky Way, and tell us new things about the Universe.

South Pole Telescope

Although there is ice everywhere, the South Pole is very dry. This makes it the perfect place to use a telescope to look for signals from the second the Universe began.

South Pole Telescope

Aurora Australis

There are times when the sky above the polar regions glows with shimmering blue, green, red and purple light. This spectacular lightshow in the Southern Hemisphere is known as the Aurora Australis.

The Amundsen–Scott South Pole Station is home to about 150 scientists and other workers in summer, and 50 people in winter.

The First Light

Almost 14 billion years ago, our Universe burst into existence in an explosion we call the Big Bang. The light from the Big Bang has been recorded by the South Pole Telescope.

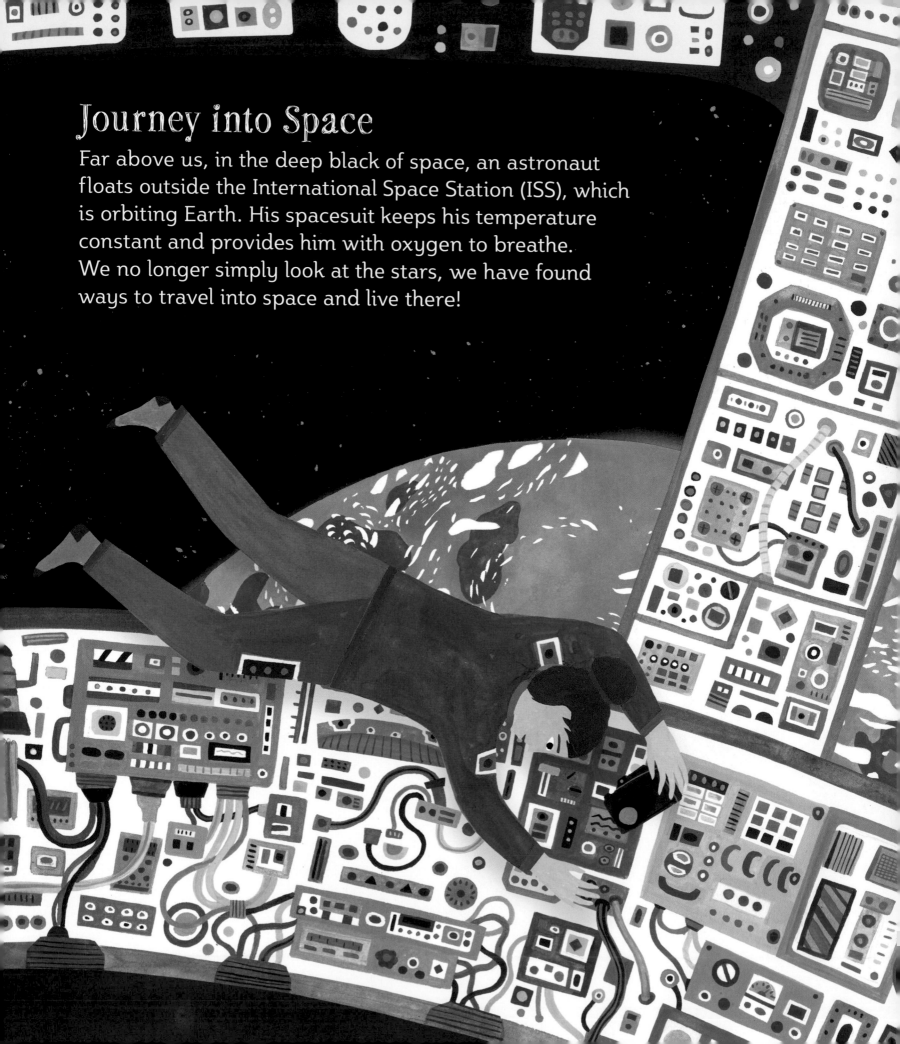

Journey into Space

Far above us, in the deep black of space, an astronaut floats outside the International Space Station (ISS), which is orbiting Earth. His spacesuit keeps his temperature constant and provides him with oxygen to breathe. We no longer simply look at the stars, we have found ways to travel into space and live there!

The International Space Station

In 1961, Russian cosmonaut Yuri Gagarin was the first person to leave Earth and travel into space. Today, up to six astronauts live and work on the ISS all year round. Look up and you may even see the ISS. It's the third brightest object in the night sky and from Earth it looks like a fast-moving star or aeroplane.

The James Webb Space Telescope will travel 1.5 million kilometres away from Earth, to explore distant galaxies in our Universe.

When an astronaut leaves the ISS to conduct repairs, it is called a spacewalk.

Where Are We?

How do astronauts or robots in space find a direction without an earthly compass? GPS works on Earth, but not in space. The answer is the same as it was for sailors thousands of years ago – by looking at the stars.

Animals and the Night Sky

Animals, birds and insects use the night sky too. Every year, millions of creatures travel vast distances in search of food, warmth, or to breed. How do they know where they're going? They look for landmarks such as rivers, mountains and forests, following the twinkling stars.

Indigo Bunting

When winter approaches, these North American birds rise into the sky, and set off on a 3,000-kilometre journey to South America. Indigo bunting fly by night and are guided by the stars.

North Star

Guiding Lights

Some animals have a built-in compass to help them find their way. Others use the light of the Moon, the North Star or Betelgeuse, which is a bright star in the constellation Orion.

Night Flights

Every year, yellow underwing moths take flight on powdery wings, moving with the seasons. To help navigate they use their internal compass, and the wind and light from the night sky. These are all the tools they need!

Stargazing

Above the glare of millions of streetlights, the stars continue to shine. New stars are being born all the time, and moons are circling distant planets. Right at this very moment, satellites are orbiting Earth and dust from space is falling through the atmosphere like a thousand fireflies.

Bright lights make it difficult to see starlight. If you can, turn out the lights and allow your eyes to adjust, so you can see the stars!

Meteor Shower

Have you ever seen a shower of bright neon lights falling through the night sky? We call these shooting stars, but actually it's a meteor shower. Meteors are small pieces of rock or specks of dust that glow as they fall through Earth's atmosphere.

Amazing Stars

On a clear night, go outside with an adult to stargaze. Bring a compass so you can find north, and a star map to help you identify the stars. You'll be amazed at what you can see! When you look up, think of all those people across history who have looked up before you, and gazed at the same stars that you see.